INTERACTIVE WORKBOOK

watch your mouth

TONY EVANS

HARVEST HOUSE PUBLISHERS
EUGENE, OREGON

Cover by Troy Black

WATCH YOUR MOUTH INTERACTIVE WORKBOOK
Copyright © 2016 Tony Evans
Published by Harvest House Publishers
Eugene, Oregon 97402
www.harvesthousepublishers.com

ISBN 978-0-7369-6772-3 (pbk.)

Printed in the United States of America

18 19 20 21 22 23 24 / VP-JC / 10 9 8 7

contents

Making the Most of This Interactive Workbook

This *Interactive Workbook* is a tool to help your group combine the *Watch Your Mouth* video and Bible study into a dynamic growth experience. If you are the leader or facilitator of your group, take some time in advance to consider the questions in the Video Group Discussion and Group Bible Exploration portions of this guide and come up with personal examples to encourage discussion. To get the most out of this study, each group member should have their own *Interactive Workbook*. This will allow them to take notes during the group time as well as dig deeper on their own throughout the week.

Every group session includes a video portion, so think about the logistics in advance. Will everyone be able to see the screen clearly? Make sure to set the audio at a comfortable level before the session. You don't want your group to miss anything.

With that in mind, let's preview the guide. Each lesson has six sections.

Video Teaching Notes

Several key points and quotes from the video are provided in this section, but there's also room to write down your own notes. Each video session will include real-life stories as well as teaching from Tony Evans.

Video Group Discussion

People can forget the content unless they review it right away. Many of the discussion questions have to do with remembering what they just viewed. But other questions try to connect the video to their emotions or experience. *How did you feel when they said that? Is that true in your life? Do you have the same issue?*

Group Bible Exploration

This is a Bible study, so each session is grounded in Scripture. Within your group, you may find different levels of faith. This is a time to open up the Bible and grow as a group or help others find their faith.

In Closing

The goal for every Bible study is to apply what you've learned. This section will highlight the main point of the lesson and challenge your group to spend some time in the coming week diving deeper into this week's theme.

On Your Own Between Sessions

This section includes additional study individuals can do to keep the content they just learned fresh in their minds throughout the week and put it into practice.

Recommended Reading

Your group time in this video Bible study will be enhanced if everyone takes the time to read the recommended chapters in *Watch Your Mouth* by Tony Evans. Tony's video teaching follows the book, but there is considerably more information and illustrations in the book. If you are the leader, encourage your group to prepare ahead as well.

Session
1

Who Is Master of Your Mouth?

As I began to compile my notes to teach and write on this topic of our words, I was interested to see how very little had been previously taught or written on the subject. That amazed me because there is precious little in our lives that carries such an enormous impact on our lives. Just like physical life and death are contained in the power of the heart, life and death—whether emotional, relational, spiritual or even physical—are contained in the power of the tongue. We certainly would never downplay the role our heart has in our lives, and yet this subject of speech doesn't seem to get the airtime it deserves in Christian realms. Especially when it makes such a crucial contribution to our success or failure, individually and collectively.

Watch Your Mouth, page 32

Video Teaching Notes

As you watch the video, use the space below to take notes. Some key points and quotes are provided here as reminders.

Jarid's Story

Jarid grew up without a father, and he developed a bad habit of lying to people to get want he wanted. He served in the air force and enjoyed riding motorcycles and shooting guns in his spare time. He lived a wild lifestyle, partying, drinking, and sleeping with women. He had a short temper, and his words often got him in trouble. He frequently shouted at people when he got mad. He struggled to hold down a job because of his angry outbursts at his bosses.

Jarid started going to church, but he was embarrassed about being unemployed. He lied about being a New York City firefighter, and when he was called out on it, many people stopped trusting him. He realized that he had a bad habit of lying and that he needed to work on that because he was now following the Lord. Listen to Jarid's testimony and pay close attention to his heart as he explains how his words brought pain to himself and those around him, and how he had to rebuild what his own mouth had torn down.

Teaching 1: Tony Evans

1. Dynamite is a powerful tool for good and for bad. What are some ways dynamite has been used for good in our nation's history? What are some ways it is used for bad?

2. How does dynamite compare to the use of the mouth? In what ways can the same mouth be used for good and for bad?

3. How is the tragedy of death in the Garden of Eden tied to words?

The mouth can be used to...

    build up or tear down

    encourage or deceive

    create or destroy

Quotables

- You and I were created by God with access to an internal, explosive power that can construct or destroy.

- This tool is the dynamite in our dentures—the tool known as the tongue.

- Your greatest enemy is in your own mouth. So is your greatest friend.

- Whoever controls your tongue controls your life.

Stacy's Story

Stacy's daughter Ellie was born missing 65 percent of her brain's left hemisphere. Ellie's doctors told Stacy and her husband that Ellie would never walk, talk, or perform any meaningful behavior. Stacy asked God to help her accept this devastating news for her daughter, but she felt God prompting her to not give up—to pray in faith, trusting God to heal Ellie. Stacy and her husband and their church prayed in faith not only for Ellie's healing but also that God would be glorified through Ellie's life. Today, Ellie is a fully functioning 12-year-old girl. She walks, talks, reads on the same level as her peers, and likes to swim and dance.

Teaching 2: Tony Evans

Jesus cursed a fig tree because it was not producing fruit. Within 24 hours, the entire fig tree had withered.

The disciples wanted to know how Jesus could affect a tree with just His words.

Jesus assured them they could do that and more by speaking to (not about) the mountain they were facing. He told them that after they spoke to the mountain, they were to speak to God about it.

Use words to face challenges in life by...

1. finding out what God says on the matter in His Word

2. speaking God's truth directly to the situation you are facing

3. holding God hostage to His Word and His character when you speak to Him about it

4. reminding yourself of God's truth

Video Group Discussion

1. What did you learn from the examples of Jarid and Stacy? What negative results happened from the use of their mouths? What positive results happened? How important is it to be honest in your relationships with each other and also with God?

2. We encounter various situations in life where we are tempted to use our mouths for negative things such as complaining or gossiping. Did Jesus complain about the fig

tree, or did He address it? What is the difference between those two approaches with our speech?

3. God's call to Moses to use his mouth and words to lead the people of Israel to freedom was a divine direction to his destiny. In what way has the Lord spoken to you about your destiny? Are you dependent on Him for accomplishing any of it? In what areas are you most dependent on Him?

4. How would you describe the difference between the "life in the tongue" and "death in the tongue"? Describe how someone might exemplify one kind or the other.

5. On the continuum below, where would you put your own mouth? Put an X at that spot.

Death--Life

Where do you think you were, say, ten years ago? Put an O at that spot, and then draw an arrow from the O to the X. What's your trend? Are you growing and maturing in your mouth, staying the same, or going backward?

6. Moses was obedient to God and used his mouth to lead his people into a better future. As you think about the possibilities in your own life, is there a particular way you can use your words to help others? It could be through blogging, teaching a Sunday school class, singing in the church choir, visiting nursing homes, writing inspirational social media posts, writing a book...any number of ways. Share how God might be leading you to use your mouth and your words for Him.

Group Bible Exploration

A grocery clerk was asked by a lady if she could buy half a head of lettuce. He replied, "Half a head? That would be very difficult—lettuce grows as whole heads, so that's how we sell them."

"You mean," she persisted, "that after all the years I've shopped here, you won't sell me half a head of lettuce?"

The man paused to consider her request and then offered to ask the manager on her behalf. Smiling with appreciation, the woman watched the young man go to the front of the store and ask for the manager.

The young man had to wait a minute before the manager was available to talk, but then he said, "You won't believe this, but there's a lame-brained lady back there who wants to know if she can buy half a head of lettuce. What do you say?"

As he spoke, the clerk noticed the manager gesturing for him to stop. Realizing he was nudging him to be aware of what was behind him, he turned around and saw the lady standing right there. Instead of waiting, she had decided to go find out the answer for herself.

The young clerk simply turned back to the manager and said, "And this nice lady was wondering if she could buy the other half."

Later in the day, the manager approached his young clerk and asked him where he had learned to think on his feet so quickly. Grateful the clerk had saved a customer through his way with words, the manager wanted to know where he had acquired such a skill.

"I grew up in Grand Rapids," the man stated. "And if you know anything about Grand Rapids, you know it's known for its great hockey teams and its ugly women."

The manager's face flushed. "My wife is from Grand Rapids."

The clerk promptly replied, "Which hockey team did she play for?"

Words can get us into trouble, and they can also get us out of trouble. But one of the greatest pieces of wisdom in the Bible lets us know that when we refrain from speaking altogether, we are choosing the better way—most of the time.

Read Together Proverbs 17:28 (NASB)

Even a fool, when he keeps silent, is considered wise; when he closes his lips, he is considered prudent.

1. This verse tells us that even someone who is considered to be a fool can appear to be wise if he or she simply remains silent. What else can we surmise from this verse about the value of silence and verbal restraint?

2. If a fool can appear wise when he or she is silent, what does that say about someone who is discerning and seeking to live a godly life?

3. Give some practical examples of when it would be prudent not to speak what is on your mind.

4. How does this apply to social media? (Keep in mind, words you post on social media are like words you speak. Written words come from the same place as spoken words—your heart.)

5. Sometimes people appear to be sincere and Christlike—until they say or post something that reveals their true motivations. Please do *not* share any names, but have you seen this happen? If so, how did the experience make you feel? What did you learn about your own life and speech?

Read Together Deuteronomy 30:19

I call heaven and earth as witnesses against you today that I have set before you life and death, blessing and curse. So choose life so that you and your descendants may live.

1. When Moses says "life and death," is he referring to people physically living or dying? Or is he referring to bringing a blessing or destruction through their choices and their words? Explain your answer and discuss how we can bring about blessings or curses through our mouths.

Life is the enjoyment of the favor of God. Death is the removal of divine favor, leading to the death of a dream, the death of a relationship, or whatever. The same tool in your mouth can bring both. In a surgeon's skilled hand, a scalpel can help preserve life, but a criminal can use the same sharpened blade to bring death. A wise doctor can use a syringe to promote healing in a sick patient, but a drug pusher can use the same syringe to cause death.

Watch Your Mouth, page 7

2. Give an example of how the mouth can be used for good but also for bad. If you are willing, share an example from your own life and how it affected those around you.

Take a moment to read the following verses out loud.

Proverbs 6:2

Proverbs 15:4

Proverbs 12:18

Proverbs 13:3

3. Summarize all four verses by creating a brand-new proverb (or word of wisdom) that contrasts the two uses of speech. Take a moment to craft your proverb and then write it down. Go around the room and give each person an opportunity to share his or her proverb.

4. Based on Proverbs 6:2 (above), what is an example of how our words can "trap" us? What would be a wise way to avoid this in the future?

5. When God wanted to create something, He used words. When Satan wanted to destroy something, he used words. Both God and Satan used words to exercise their power. Since the tool of your tongue is so incredibly powerful, you can imagine why there is a fight in your mouth between God and the devil. There is a war for your words because life and death come through your words. In what ways can Satan fight to influence your mouth? Keep in mind that the words reflect the heart. In what ways can you seek to guard your heart from negative influences?

Read Together Psalm 141:3

LORD, set up a guard for my mouth; keep watch at the door of my lips.

1. What does a guard do?

2. In what way can God set a guard over our mouths?

3. How easy is it to ignore this guard? What emotions or thoughts would motivate you to ignore this guard?

4. Sometimes people use the word "vent" when they feel the need to complain for a long time. If the Lord set a guard for your mouth, would that guard encourage you to vent?

5. Can you think of a biblical example of Jesus "venting" (complaining only for the sake of getting His emotions or frustrations out)? Or did Jesus appear to speak harsh words only for a specific purpose?

Read Together James 1:26

If anyone thinks he is religious without controlling his tongue, then his religion is useless and he deceives himself.

1. What are some things we might do as believers that James would consider "religious"?

2. Do you think it is extreme to say that these things are "useless" when we do not tame our tongue?

3. Why are the mouth and the words we say so critical in supporting a Christlike spirituality in our lives? What does our tongue reveal about our heart and our spirit?

4. On the scale below, mark where you believe you are with regard to taming your tongue (10 being the most tamed and 1 being not tamed at all).

1--- 10

5. What steps can you take today and this week to move yourself higher on that scale, closer to a 10?

6. What is keeping you from taking those steps? (It could be fear—that if you do not voice your opinion or speak up for yourself, things may not go well. Be honest, as this is an area where everyone struggles.)

Pray right now that the Lord will give you wisdom on how to overcome what is keeping you from taking those steps.

Read Together James 3:4-6

And consider ships: Though very large and driven by fierce winds, they are guided by a very small rudder wherever the will of the pilot directs. So too, though the tongue is a small part of the body, it boasts great things. Consider how large a forest a small fire ignites. And the tongue is a fire.

1. James uses the illustration of a ship to remind us that the rudder guides the ship wherever the pilot directs it. Who should be the pilot of your tongue?

2. What are some practical ways you can yield your speech to the Lord and His will more consistently? It might mean counting to ten before you speak, allowing yourself time to think rather than react. It could mean cutting back on texting or email or social

media posts. List three ideas that will be most helpful to you, and implement them this week.

In Closing

As you end the study today, pray together for self-control with regard to your mouth. Pray also for wisdom, asking the Lord to open your eyes and your heart to what His Word truly says regarding your speech. Ask Him for the understanding to use your mouth well and not for evil.

Before session 2, complete the "On Your Own Between Sessions" section below. Consider starting the next session by asking people to share what they learned from the following exercises.

On Your Own Between Sessions

A Firestorm

The Oakland Firestorm of 1991 started as a small grass fire in the Berkeley Hills. Strong Diablo winds caused that grass fire to spread quickly. By the time it was contained, it had consumed 1520 acres as well as more than 3500 homes, apartments, and condos. This was one of the most expensive fires in the history of our nation, with damages estimated at $1.5 billion.

What had taken years to build was destroyed in only a matter of hours. The tongue can do similar damage, especially in relationships. During your personal time in this study, reflect on a situation when your words or someone else's words damaged a relationship. Ask the Lord to forgive where there was wrong and to heal what has been broken. Also ask Him to reveal any lies that Satan has planted in your mind or in the other person's mind as a result of these words, and to replace them with His truth.

Take a moment to write down any of these truths He brings to your mind as you pray.

A Tree and Its Fruit

We praise our Lord and Father with it, and we curse men who are made in God's likeness with it. Praising and cursing come out of the same mouth. My brothers, these things should not be this way. Does a spring pour out sweet and bitter water from the same opening? Can a fig tree produce olives, my brothers, or a grapevine produce figs? Neither can a saltwater spring yield fresh water (James 3:9-12).

Fill in the list with the fruit or the contents of the object. Indicate whether this fruit is good or bad.

Object	Fruit or Contents
orange tree	_____
grapevine	_____
fig tree	_____
freshwater lake	_____

Notice how each item bears fruit or has content that resembles its source. It cannot produce things outside of what it is. Yet James tells us the mouth produces both good and bad. This is because of what James calls "double-mindedness" in James 1:8 (NASB).

Look up James 1:7-8 and write the verses here.

Some characteristics of double-mindedness include compromise, shifting between peace and anxiety, giving in to unhealthy habits, and incompetence with the Word of God. Matthew 7:16-20 tells us that we can identify people by their fruit. A good tree cannot produce bad fruit, and a bad tree cannot produce good fruit.

1. What kind of tree are you, and what kind of fruit do you produce when it comes to your mouth?

2. How might the fruit you produce negatively affect those around you—especially with regard to how they view God and Christianity?

A Burning Bush

Read Exodus 4:1-13.

1. What was Moses's first response to God (verse 1)?

2. What did God do and say to demonstrate His power to Moses (verses 2-9)?

3. What was Moses's next response to God (verse 10)?

4. How did the Lord respond to Moses's claim that he could not speak (verses 11-12)?

5. Have you ever felt as if God asked you to do or say something you were not qualified for? What was your response? Many of us respond like Moses and doubt that we can accomplish what God has asked us to do. Based on God's multiple responses to Moses, how do you think He wants to respond to you?

6. Can you trust Him to be Lord of your lips and God in your gums so you can be a voice for Him in whatever area He is calling you? If so, list two specific areas where you need to depend on God to give you the words to say, and then pray that He will give you grace and wisdom in each of those situations.

Open Day Experiment

Pick a day this week to experiment with God being the Lord of your lips. Shortly after you wake up, talk with God. Indicate your desire to yield your thoughts and your words to Him and His will for His glory. Then as you go through the day—breakfast, commute, work, lunch, family time, a trip to the corner store, a visit with friends...keep this in mind. You are *willing* to let God guide your heart and your speech. You don't need to plan to say anything religious. Just be open to saying whatever God brings to your mind in any situation.

This might mean paying attention to the people around you. What needs do they have, and how can your words make a difference? How can you show them the love of Christ through what you say or do not say? It might mean taking some extra time with a friend or family member who needs to talk. Or God might throw a challenge your way. Will you face this willingly, trusting in His help and wisdom?

Experiment Follow-Up

After trying the Open Day experiment, talk about it with someone else. Was it good, weird, hard, instructive, life-changing, pointless...?

Consider talking about it when you gather for the next session of *Watch Your Mouth*.

Recommended Reading

In preparation for session 2, you may want to read chapters 5–7 of *Watch Your Mouth*. To review the material from session 1, read chapters 1–4.

Your Voice Has Victory

There are two extremes in evangelical circles when it comes to this matter of speaking to the mountains in our lives. On one hand, many evangelicals emphasize studying Scripture, learning what it says, memorizing it...but they don't teach us how to actually *speak* it. As a result, we find believers who are biblically literate but who are powerless when it comes to dealing with the adverse circumstances (the mountains) in their lives.

On the other hand, many other evangelicals so emphasize speaking to their mountains (often referred to as speaking things into existence) that they teach things that are inconsistent with God's Word, leaving them equally powerless.

So let me be clear. How can you be sure that the words you are speaking to your mountain are the words God wants you to say? How can you be confident that your faith is in God and not in your own words? Here is the key: Your words must be aligned with Scripture.

Saying whatever you want won't move mountains. And merely knowing what Scripture says won't move mountains. But you *can* overcome the big challenges in your life by speaking the truths of Scripture directly to your situation.

Watch Your Mouth, pages 62–63

Video Teaching Notes

As you watch the video, use the space below to take notes. Some key points and quotes are provided here as reminders.

Becki's Story

The future looked bleak for Becki and her husband after their daughter was murdered. But in the midst of their great pain, God gave Becki and her husband the grace to forgive the man responsible for their daughter's death. Despite their tragic circumstances, Becki and her husband chose to trust God and give Him praise for who He is and all the good He was doing, and through that they found strength and healing.

Teaching 1: Tony Evans

Jehoshaphat began his prayer by acknowledging the greatness of God.

Next, he reminded God of what He had said.

Then he invited God into the problem.

Quotables

- God's address is praise. You can locate Him through praise.
- Midnight is the darkest hour, when there is no light, no escape, no hope. But that is when you need to use your mouth the most—to praise.

Lavenia's Story

When Lavenia became a Christian, she felt a nudge to tell people that God loved them, but the responses she received were not encouraging. She pleaded to God that He would use her words to make a difference in people's lives.

One day, while driving through town, she saw a towering man standing alone at a bus stop, and she felt the urge to tell him about God's love. But she was also hesitant of what he might say or think. She pushed through her fear and told him he was loved and valued, and soon he began to sob.

Teaching 2: Tony Evans

Wisdom is the ability to navigate the twists and turns of life carefully, especially when those twists and turns bring unprecedented pain.

Wisdom is the ability to apply biblical truth to life's reality.

Get wise people around you and listen to them.

Wisdom is a person—Jesus. Abide in Christ—let His words become your thoughts.

Video Group Discussion

1. In Becki's story, we saw how God used her obedience in the face of unspeakable loss and pain to impact people's lives for good. Becki shared with us her anger toward the Lord but how He met her in that anger and let her know He understood her pain

because He had lost a child too. How important is it to know that God empathizes with us? Does that help to change your response in difficult situations?

2. We heard in the video how Jehoshaphat saw enemies on every corner. He saw no exit signs and no way out from what looked like complete defeat. Yet Jehoshaphat chose to trust in God and encourage those around him to trust in God as well. When you are struggling, how you react has an impact on those around you. In what ways can you use your words to strengthen those around you or under you, or maybe to model a right response in that situation?

3. Do you often take into account how people are looking at you when you are in a challenging situation and can be impacted positively by what you do and say? How does being aware of that affect your response?

4. Tony's teaching in the video laid out a three-part response to God with our words when we face life's challenges.

   • reminding God of who He is

   • reminding God of what He has said

   • telling God about the problem

What is one challenge you (or perhaps you and your spouse) are facing?

5. *Remind God of who He is.* What attributes of God relate specifically to your challenge? For example, if your challenge is financial, think of God as *Jehovah-Jireh*, the sovereign provider.

6. *Remind God of what He has said.* What has God said about the issue you face? For example, if the issue is rejection or loneliness, you can remind God of His promise to never leave you or forsake you. Find at least three promises in God's Word that you can remind Him about. (You could use your digital device to search "Bible verses about…")

7. *Tell God about the problem.* Now that you have reminded God of His character and His promises, tell Him about the problem you face. Ask Him to give you wisdom and direction or to simply show up in the situation. Be open to His leading. As we saw in the story of Jehoshaphat (and also in Lavenia's story), God sometimes asks us to do something we don't feel comfortable doing. But if we are obedient, He will be there with us. What might God be asking you to do?

8. How did the response from the man on the road whom Lavenia talked to about God encourage her to continue being obedient when God leads her?

9. Can you think of a time when God affirmed your obedience? What was your response?

10. In the video, Tony said when you "can't stand no more," you are to "get your praise on." In what ways can you do this?

Group Bible Exploration

Read Together 2 Chronicles 20:1-5 (NASB)

Now it came about after this that the sons of Moab and the sons of Ammon, together with some of the Meunites, came to make war against Jehoshaphat. Then some came and reported to Jehoshaphat, saying, "A great multitude is coming against you from beyond the sea, out of Aram and behold, they are in Hazazon-tamar (that is Engedi)." Jehoshaphat was afraid and turned his attention to seek the LORD, and proclaimed a fast throughout all Judah. So Judah gathered together to seek help from the LORD; they even came from all the cities of Judah to seek the LORD.

1. Describe Jehoshaphat's emotions in the face of this battle.

2. Why was he afraid? What did he choose to do with this fear?

3. Compare Jehoshaphat's response to his fear to your typical response to fear. When you are afraid, do you tend to talk more, to complain, or put down other people or yourself? How do you usually respond to fear?

4. Based on Jehoshaphat's example, what should we do when we face troubling emotions, such as fear, depression, or rejection?

5. We may not be able to proclaim a fast the way Jehoshaphat did, but have you ever asked anyone to fast for you? Or have you ever been asked to fast for someone else? What was the result? If you have not, consider doing so. Your fast, combined with your words of prayer, can make a true impact in someone's life.

Some of us, if we were honest enough, would challenge the theological dictum that God won't put more on you than you can bear. We know what it feels like to have more put on us than we can bear. We've been burdened by life's problems, whether in our finances, our health, our family, or a relationship that just keeps going from bad to worse. Or sometimes you feel stuck in a career or job and can't see a way out of your current situation. It might be an addiction that causes you to feel trapped—surrounded on all sides, just like Jehoshaphat. The enemy is converging on you, and you no longer feel any peace or stability in your life.

If you are in a situation like that or have ever been, the lessons we learn from Jehoshaphat regarding our mouth will no doubt help you immensely. The king was in a battle. He was in a war. And yet the solution to his problem—the victory he was seeking—was not found in weapons or artillery. Rather, the victory Jehoshaphat needed was found in his voice. And just as this king used his voice, you can use yours to gain access to the power you need to be victorious in the struggles of your life.

Watch Your Mouth, pages 72–73

Read Together 2 Chronicles 20:12 (NASB)

O our God, will You not judge them? For we are powerless before this great multitude who are coming against us; nor do we know what to do, but our eyes are on You.

1. What does Jehoshaphat admit in these words to God?

2. Have you ever felt powerless in a situation—at work, in a relationship, or in your finances? Describe that situation, as much as you want to share, and how you responded.

3. What are some normal ways of responding to feelings of powerlessness? Is it natural to want to defend yourself? How do we often defend ourselves with our words?

4. What does it mean, by way of actions, to turn our eyes to God in situations of powerlessness? How does that affect our mouth?

Read Together 2 Chronicles 20:6-9

Yahweh, the God of our ancestors, are You not the God who is in heaven, and do You not rule over all the kingdoms of the nations? Power and might are in Your hand, and no one can stand against You. Are You not our God who drove out the inhabitants of this land before Your people Israel and who gave it forever to the descendants of Abraham Your friend? They have lived in the land and have built You a sanctuary in it for Your name and have said, "If disaster comes on us—sword or judgment, pestilence or famine—we will stand before this temple and before You, for Your name is in this temple. We will cry out to You because of our distress, and You will hear and deliver.

1. Do you recognize or pick up on an order in this prayer?

2. How valuable is reminding God and ourselves of God's attributes and history when we are facing challenges in life? Why?

3. In what way does Jehoshaphat praise God in this prayer of supplication?

> Prayer is an invitation to heaven to address something going wrong on earth. It's calling on eternity to visit time. It's giving heavenly permission for earthly intervention. Prayer is not the pregame; it is the game. It is not the preparation for battle; it is the war. Every significant movement in the history of Christianity was birthed first and foremost in prayer. That's the approach this king took when his nation was surrounded by enemies. Jehoshaphat strategically cried out to God.
>
> *Watch Your Mouth*, page 74

Note the anatomy of the king's prayer:

- The king begins by reminding God who He is.
- Then he reminds God about what He has said.
- After this, he introduces God to the problem he is facing.

Read Together 2 Chronicles 20:14-19 (NASB)

In the midst of the assembly the Spirit of the LORD came upon Jahaziel the son of Zechariah, the son of Benaiah, the son of Jeiel, the son of Mattaniah, the Levite of the sons of Asaph; and he said, "Listen, all Judah and the inhabitants of Jerusalem and King Jehoshaphat: thus says the LORD to you, 'Do not fear or be dismayed because of this great multitude, for the battle is not yours but God's. Tomorrow go down against them. Behold, they will come up by the ascent of Ziz, and you will find them at the end of the valley in front of the wilderness of Jeruel. You need not fight in this battle; station yourselves, stand and see the salvation of the LORD on your behalf, O Judah and Jerusalem.' Do not fear or be dismayed; tomorrow go out to face them, for the LORD is with you."

Jehoshaphat bowed his head with his face to the ground, and all Judah and the inhabitants of Jerusalem fell down before the LORD, worshiping the LORD. The Levites, from the sons of the Kohathites and of the sons of the Korahites, stood up to praise the LORD God of Israel, with a very loud voice.

1. How did God ask the people to respond to the battle they were facing?

2. Is this a normal or typical battle plan?

3. Imagine how the people must have felt given such a plan. Now contrast that with how they responded to the plan in praising God. What did their praise demonstrate?

4. Imagine yourself facing what looks like certain defeat—and God telling you not to fight, not to defend yourself, not to do anything but stand and station yourself. Do you think you could respond in praise? Or would you be more likely to give Him praise only after you see Him win the victory?

5. God says He is a rewarder of our faith. Our praise before a victory demonstrates our faith. How might you incorporate this mindset into your lifestyle on a more regular basis?

Read Together 2 Chronicles 20:20-23 (NASB)

They rose early in the morning and went out to the wilderness of Tekoa; and when they went out, Jehoshaphat stood and said, "Listen to me, O Judah and inhabitants of Jerusalem, put your trust in the LORD your God and you will be established. Put your trust in His prophets and succeed." When he had consulted with the people, he appointed those who sang to the LORD and those who praised Him in holy attire, as they went out before the army and said, "Give thanks to the Lord, for His lovingkindness is everlasting." When they began singing and praising, the LORD set ambushes against the sons of Ammon, Moab and Mount Seir, who had come against Judah; so they were routed. For the sons of Ammon and Moab rose up against the inhabitants of Mount Seir destroying them completely; and when they had finished with the inhabitants of Seir, they helped to destroy one another.

1. What happened when the people began to praise God?

2. Describe a specific situation in your life or in the life of someone you know where you can use this strategy of praising God in faith. Ask the Lord for the wisdom to know whether that is what He wants you to do in this particular case. Give Him the fruit of your lips and watch Him move in response to your faith.

3. Twice in this passage we read, "Put your trust in…" And once we read, "Give thanks." What is the correlation between trust and gratitude? How are they often linked?

In Closing

As you end the study today, pray together for the ability to trust God in faith and to praise Him in times of trial and testing. Perhaps some in the group want to share their personal challenges on a deeper level—what areas can you affect positively through your words of faith and praise? Ask God for insight, for discernment, and for the courage to praise.

Before session 3, complete the "On Your Own Between Sessions" section below. Consider reviewing that section at the beginning of session 3.

On Your Own Between Sessions
Wisdom in the Book of Proverbs

- "The tongue of the wise makes knowledge attractive,
  but the mouth of fools blurts out foolishness" (15:2).

- "The tongue that heals is a tree of life,
  but a devious tongue breaks the spirit" (15:4).

- "The lips of the wise broadcast knowledge,
  but not so the heart of fools" (15:7).

- "Wisdom is found on the lips of the discerning,
  but a rod is for the back of the one who lacks sense.
  The wise store up knowledge,
  but the mouth of the fool hastens destruction" (10:13-14).

- "When there are many words, sin is unavoidable,
  but the one who controls his lips is wise.
  The tongue of the righteous is pure silver;
  the heart of the wicked is of little value.
  The lips of the righteous feed many,
  but fools die for lack of sense" (10:19-21).

1. These verses and many others make clear that if you could be wiser with your speech, life would be better. Talk better, and you will live better. Why do you think sin is unavoidable when there are many words?

2. What is the meaning of the word "discernment"? How can you incorporate more discernment into your life, thoughts, and words?

3. Scripture tells us that the wise "store up knowledge." Are you making every effort to add to your biblical knowledge on a regular basis? In what ways could you even improve on this?

4. Summarize from the verses what happens when you lack wisdom in your words.

Being Wise and Being Smart

1. Wisdom involves more than being smart. You can have multiple degrees and still be a fool. Wisdom is the ability to see beyond the obvious and make choices that reflect the highest good for everyone involved, including yourself. How does wisdom differ from simply being smart?

2. Look up Proverbs 18:6. What does a lack of wisdom in your words lead to?

3. Have you ever experienced this in your own life—not a beating, but some kind of destruction in your work or a relationship—due to unwise words? If so, what did you learn from that situation?

4. Look up and read James 1:5. Write it out in your own words.

The Gift of Wisdom

1. How often do you ask the Lord for wisdom? Should you increase this frequency?

2. Take time right now to ask God to give you wisdom related to specific situations in your life. Write down these situations and continue to ask God each day, hour, minute—however often He reminds you or you think of it—to give you wisdom. Write down in the other column what He tells you through either His Spirit, a confirming message, or His Word.

Situation One   Wisdom from God

_____   _____

Situation Two   Wisdom from God

_____   _____

Situation Three   Wisdom from God

_____   _____

Words That Build

1. On your own or with your spouse, recall some things you have said that may not have been wise. It could have been things you said to each other. Confess these things and ask the Lord to give you wisdom in your speech moving forward. Wisdom is a priceless gift from God that far too often goes unopened.

2. Read the following verses.

   - "So then, we must pursue what promotes peace and what builds up one another" (Romans 14:19).
   - "All things must be done for edification" (1 Corinthians 14:26).
   - "From Him the whole body, fitted and knit together by every supporting ligament, promotes the growth of the body for building up itself in love by the proper working of each individual part" (Ephesians 4:16).
   - "Encourage one another and build each other up as you are already doing" (1 Thessalonians 5:11).

   Based on these verses, how important is it to use our mouths to build each other up? Write down three specific people you are going to be intentional about building up this month with your words. Write yourself reminders if need be. And don't forget to build yourself up with God's words of truth about your value and identity in Him.

Recommended Reading

In preparation for session 3, you may want to read chapters 8 and 9 of *Watch Your Mouth*.

Your Mouth Mirrors Your Heart

This emotional response to how great God is ought to be one of the primary uses of our mouths. "I will praise the LORD at all times; His praise will always be on my lips" (Psalm 34:1). The NASB puts it this way: "His praise shall continually be in my mouth." How often is continually? All the time. After all, how often does God give you breath? So it makes sense that our praise of Him should comprise the greatest volume of what comes out of our mouths.

God wants to be blessed by your lips. He wants to hear your gratitude and thanksgiving. You bless Him when you remember what He has done for you and express your appreciation to Him and to others.

Watch Your Mouth, page 112

Video Teaching Notes

As you watch the video, use the space below to take notes. Some key points and quotes are provided here as reminders.

Crystal's Story

Despite growing up in a Christian home, Crystal endured a lot: a difficult divorce, a home foreclosure, a job layoff, and the struggle of being a newly single mother. She felt as if her life in New York was crumbling. She moved to Texas with hopes to start over, and her neighbor spoke a timely, encouraging word to Crystal: "God is going to turn your mourning into joy." She received it and began to live it out. She started investing in her church and community, she began serving, she remarried, and she is currently experiencing a new level of faith and joy.

Teaching 1: Tony Evans

First Thessalonians 5:18 (NASB) says, "In everything give thanks." It doesn't say, "For everything." In the middle of whatever you're going through, find the things for which you ought to be grateful.

Rather than complaining, make a list of all the things in your life for which you ought to be grateful.

Grab a journal or tablet and start making a note every time you complain. See how many times you do it in one day. Try even one hour. If you add thoughts to that list, you can truly gauge your heart.

Quotables

- One of the great sins in the Bible is ingratitude.
- "I complained that I had no shoes until I saw a man who had no feet."

Mike's Story

Prior to coming to Christ, Mike had a filthy mouth. He cursed like a sailor, called his coworkers stupid, and filled his conversation with sexual innuendos, inappropriate comments to women at work, and the like. When Mike came to Christ, people immediately noticed a change in his speech. He lifted people up and encouraged them rather than tearing them down, and this led to important conversations about Jesus's power over the tongue.

Teaching 2: Tony Evans

God can change your speech when He changes your heart.

What is in your heart shows up in your speech. Just as the tongue reveals whether a patient is healthy or sick, our words reveal whether our hearts are spiritually mature or weak.

God has a wiretap on our mouths. He's picking up everything we say, and we will be held accountable for our words.

Ask God to transform your heart and your thoughts, and your speech will follow.

Video Group Discussion

1. In the video, we heard how one person's words to Crystal completely changed the outlook of her life. Crystal later used her mouth to speak life into someone else's dismal situation. Did you realize that words can have such an impact on someone else? Has anyone else's words impacted you so greatly? Will you share about this with the others in the group?

2. We saw in Mike's story that when his heart changed, his words changed. Not only that, but the way he received other people's words changed as well. He was no longer willing to accept being called stupid because he knew his value before God. Has anyone in your life spoken to you in a manner unworthy of who you are? How did you handle that situation? If you are still in that situation, what can you do to help change it?

3. What did Tony mean when he shared the example of his dog growling at him? How can we apply that lesson to our everyday lives?

4. Have you ever experienced someone being ungrateful to you despite all you have done for them? Did that motivate you to do more for them, or less?

   How can knowing that help you in showing God gratitude?

5. Tony spoke of two types of judgment—condemning judgment and congratulatory judgment. What kinds of things can you say to bring about the latter? What should you avoid saying so you won't receive condemning judgment?

   In the columns below, write phrases that exemplify the two categories of speech.

Condemning Judgment	Congratulatory Judgment
_____	_____
_____	_____
_____	_____

6. Toward the end of the video, Tony mentioned the meditations of our heart. Do you spend time intentionally meditating on positive, truth-based themes? Or do you allow into your heart whatever comes at you in life? How can you be more intentional about what you let into your heart? List two ways you can develop the habit of meditating on positive truth more frequently, and then seek to implement both.

Group Bible Exploration

Read Together 1 Thessalonians 5:18 (NASB)

In everything give thanks; for this is God's will for you in Christ Jesus.

1. It's a little word—only two letters. But it means a lot. We are told to give thanks "in" everything. That does not mean you have to give thanks "for" everything. Why would you give thanks "in" everything? Because it demonstrates faith in God that He can and will work out all things together for His good to those who love Him and are called according to His purpose (Romans 8:28).

   Can you name a situation in which you initially did not want to give thanks, but you eventually found a way to give thanks? Did this impact your emotions or the way you handled the situation?

2. In the video, Tony reminds us that when we are in situations that are not happy or calm, we are to look back and remember times when God has been there for us. How has God provided for you or guided you in a time when you really needed Him a lot? How has He brought you through things to the point where you are today?

3. When you think on these things and discuss them together, what emotions arise in your spirit?

Go ahead and thank God for all He has done for you and for each other.

Read Together 1 Timothy 4:4 (NASB)

For everything created by God is good, and nothing is to be rejected if it is received with gratitude.

1. Based on this verse, how important is gratitude? What role does it play in how we receive things from the Lord?

2. In what ways can you show or express gratitude when you receive something?

Aesop, the ancient storyteller, told this fable: Once upon a time, a donkey found a lion's skin. He tried it on, strutted around, and frightened many animals. Soon a fox came along, and the donkey tried to scare him too. But the fox, hearing the donkey's voice, said, "If you want to terrify me, you'll have to disguise your bray." Aesop's moral: Clothes may disguise a fool, but his words will give him away.

Read Together Matthew 12:35 (NASB)

The good man brings out of his good treasure what is good; and the evil man brings out of his evil treasure what is evil.

1. How can our words give others a picture of us?

2. Have you ever observed someone whose words did not reflect his or her outer being? Without naming names, describe what this was like.

3. Knowing that our words give us away so easily, how much attention should we pay to what we say?

4. Have you ever posted something on social media that got such a negative response that you took it down? If so, why did you decide to take it down? What did you learn about future posts or things you say?

Read Together Psalm 19:14

Let the words of my mouth and the meditation of my heart be acceptable in Your sight, O Lord, my rock and my Redeemer.

1. How could this verse change what you say? If you used this verse as a filter for everything you said, wrote, texted, or posted, would it have any effect?

2. Before you speak, text, write, or post, try pausing and asking yourself and God if what you are about to share is pleasing to Him. Let this verse guide you into righteous speech and protect you on the day the Lord judges what has come from your mouth.

Quotables

- It would be better to leave people wondering why you didn't talk than why you did.
- When all is said and done, there's a lot more said than done.
- Better to remain silent and be thought a fool than to open your mouth and remove all doubt.

Read Together Luke 6:45

A good man produces good out of the good storeroom of his heart. An evil man produces evil out of the evil storeroom, for his mouth speaks from the overflow of the heart.

1. What is produced out of the storeroom of a good man's heart?

2. What comes out of our mouth based on this verse?

3. The heart overflows into our speech. This truth underlines the importance of pursuing and maintaining a pure heart. What steps can you take to purify your heart at an even greater level than it is now?

4. Share a time when you tried to conceal your true thoughts or feelings about a matter but your speech betrayed you. What could you have done differently to avoid this?

In Closing

As you end the study today, take a moment to quiet yourself and get to the *heart* level. A better title for *Watch Your Mouth* might have been *Watch Your Heart*. Out of our heart flows our speech.

Pray together David's words from Psalm 19: "May the words of my mouth and the meditation of my heart be acceptable to You, Lord, my rock and my Redeemer."

Before session 4, complete the "On Your Own Between Sessions" section below. You might want to review that section at the beginning of session 4.

On Your Own Between Sessions

A Grateful Heart

An elderly lady is standing on the beach, watching her grandson play in the shallow water, when suddenly a huge wave sweeps the boy away. The grandmother holds her hands to the sky and screams, "Lord, how could You? Have I not been a wonderful mother and grandmother? Have I not given to You throughout my years? Have I not tried my very best to live a life You would be proud of?"

A moment later another huge wave brings the boy back, safe and sound.

The grandmother responds, "Thank You, God...but where's his hat?"

Sometimes no matter what God does, some people are just not satisfied. It's easy to recognize ungratefulness in other people but more difficult to spot it in ourselves. Take a moment to think of some things you haven't thanked God for because they aren't quite as you wanted or expected them to be. List them in the space here and then be sure to thank God for all He has done.

A New Perspective

When asked to list what he was thankful for, one little boy wrote, "My glasses!"

"That's good," said the teacher, "they help you see better."

"Actually," responded the child, "I'm thankful for my glasses because they keep the other boys from hitting me and the girls from kissing me."

This little guy clearly understood the meaning of gratitude.

Gratitude is seeing beyond what we see. It is seeing the intention behind what God does or does not do. Have you ever prayed for something, only to discover later on that you are grateful God did *not* give you what you wanted? These times help to build and strengthen our faith and trust in His sovereignty.

1. Read Isaiah 45:9-10 and write a response that incorporates the purpose of gratitude.

2. How does understanding God's sovereignty help you to trust more and increase your gratitude?

3. List some things in your life for which you do not regularly show gratitude. Ask the Lord to open your eyes to see more clearly (like the boy with his glasses) what you have to be grateful for.

Receiving Good Things from God

Take some quiet time this week to let your trust rest deeply in these truths: You are a child of the King. He desires to give you good things. A complaining and ungrateful heart negates a significant amount of the good He does for us.

During your meditation time, write down any thoughts that God brings to your mind of things for which you can be grateful. Ask Him to continue to open your heart to see the spiritual perspective behind all He is doing and has done for you. Let God speak truth deep into your heart.

Notes of Gratitude

Sticky notes can be messy sometimes. But this week let's turn sticky notes into a gift. Buy a packet of sticky notes. Challenge yourself to write 30 different gratitude statements on them to surprise people with. You can leave them at the kitchen table, on a coworker's desk, on the mailbox—any number of places. Be sure to use all 30 as you put the gift of gratitude to work for you.

An Exercise of Gratitude

This week, be intentional about being grateful. Whether it is to the store clerk, a family member, a coworker...whoever it is, express gratitude with your words on an ongoing basis. Try to take note of how that may impact your overall attitude this week.

Each time you feel like complaining this week, write down the occasion and the words "I feel like complaining." But don't write the complaint. At the end of the week, count up how many complaints you were able to stop yourself from making and thank God for giving you self-control to do so.

Recommended Reading

In preparation for session 4, read chapters 10–12 of *Watch Your Mouth*.

The Wreckage of Words

How can you tell when your talk is not what it ought to be? One identifying factor is its effect on other people. Does what you say pull people down or build them up? Do the words from your mouth inspire or destroy? After people spend time with you, do they walk away with a smile on their face and pep in their step, or do they walk away with their head hung down, their energy drained, and the light lost from their eyes?

Many of us don't realize the negative effect our words have on other people. At work, whenever someone has an idea or shares a vision, some people respond with ten reasons why it could never work. Others always look tired, and their words reflect a spirit of apathy or criticism. Still others always seem to focus attention on themselves regardless of the topic of conversation. In each case, a roomful of people can be adversely affected by one person's inappropriate words.

Words matter—they can give us enthusiasm or deplete it. They can give us hope or crush it. They can protect our reputations or destroy them.

Watch Your Mouth, pages 136–137

Video Teaching Notes

As you watch the video, use the space below to take notes. Some key points and quotes are provided here as reminders.

Eloise's Story

Eloise and her nine brothers and sisters grew up as a pastor's kids. They learned from their father how Christian community was *supposed* to function, but the congregation did nothing but judge and slander her family. After years of hearing people talk poorly about their father, many of Eloise's siblings decided never to go back to church. It hurts Eloise to know that the slander and gossip of other Christians had such a traumatic effect on her family and her faith. In her adulthood, Eloise has confronted several people from the church in order to forgive and move on without bitterness.

Teaching 1: Tony Evans

Spreading a message of gossip is like scattering feathers in the wind. Once it is sent, you can't get it back.

Slander breaks fellowship with God.

We are told not to associate with those who slander.

Flattery is like a chocolate-covered lie.

Flattery involves saying things that make others feel good just so you can accomplish your own agenda.

Evil speech, evil in our communication, whether it's gossip, or slander, or flattery, goes against God as a God of truth.

Quotables

- There can be evil in your esophagus and Satan in your speech.
- A sharp tongue is the only edged tool that grows keener with constant use (Washington Irving).

Travis's Story

Travis worked in Chicago with inner-city kids, and some of the younger guys he worked with noticed the way he talked, the language he used, and the music he listened to. They asked him why he never said certain words, and he was able to share why and how his faith influenced his speech.

One time Travis challenged a kid named Olando to a game of basketball. They agreed that if Travis won, Olando would replace the rap music on his mp3 player with worship music. Travis did win—and Olando ended up really liking the new music! Gradually, it started to change what came out of his mouth.

Teaching 2: Tony Evans

Hallow the Lord's name. Do not use it casually, in jesting or in cursing.

We should be known for speech that is clean, not filthy.

We are to bless those who curse us. Not because *they* deserve a blessing but because *we* do.

God wants us to use some spiritual mouthwash and get the dirt out of our discourse.

Video Group Discussion
Eloise

1. Eloise's father was a pastor for 50 years. At one point in the church's life, a severe division led to a tremendous amount of slander and gossip about her father. This caused a couple of her brothers to leave not only that church, but the church altogether. Why do you think these negative words had such an impact on Eloise's brothers?

2. What was Eloise's father's response? In what way did that model to her a right response to negative speech?

Travis

1. Travis told us how his example of friendship with urban youth provided opportunities to positively impact their speech. In what way did Travis refrain from judging those he was with? How did he model positive speech?

2. One of the youth lost a basketball game, and as a result, he agreed to listen to gospel and worship music. What did Travis say this resulted in with regard to the youth's own speech over time?

3. Are you mindful of the music you listen to? Do you think it impacts your own speech at all?

4. Do you feel convicted to change any of the music or television programs you allow into your heart and mind? If so, in what way?

Put-Downs

Tony shares the story of a constant battle between Winston Churchill and Lady Astor. They were in the British Parliament together, and Lady Astor said to Winston, "Sir, if you were my husband, I'd put arsenic in your tea."

Churchill replied, "If you were my wife, I'd drink it."

1. Have you ever known someone who can always "one-up" a negative word? They are quick on their feet when it comes to putting someone else down. How do you respond in the company of someone who often puts you down?

2. Does it bother you to be around people who tend to put other people down? How does that make you feel? What does that reveal about their heart?

Many times, people with an insecure heart need to put other people down. When we come to realize that we are revealing weaknesses in our own lives by insulting others, we may have more self-control in what we say.

The Telephone Game

Tony compares gossip to the telephone game. He says words can get misconstrued when someone passes a message to another person, who passes on to the next person, and so on. By the time you get to the end of the line, the message is totally different from how it started, and the truth has become distorted.

Let's take a moment to play the telephone game. Have one person write down a three-sentence statement. This person whispers the statement to the next person, and so on. (You can whisper it only once on your turn.) At the end of the line or circle, the last person repeats what is said, and that is compared to the written statement.

Typically the words and phrases get twisted and turned by the time they reach the last person. As you can imagine, life is no different. As gossip spreads and the original source is out of the picture, the story can completely change into something it wasn't at the beginning.

Gossip is wrong at the beginning, and it becomes worse as it goes on because it becomes more and more distorted—often worse than you could have imagined.

Read Together Psalm 109:17-20 (NASB)

He also loved cursing, so it came to him;
And he did not delight in blessing, so it was far from him.
But he clothed himself with cursing as with his garment,
And it entered into his body like water
And like oil into his bones.
Let it be to him as a garment with which he covers himself,
And for a belt with which he constantly girds himself.
Let this be the reward of my accusers from the LORD.

Look again at the first line. It said that cursing came to him. Tony said that when you curse (or speak badly of) another person, this will then come back to you. How does this impact you and your speech? What spiritual effects does your speech have on you?

Group Bible Exploration

Read Together Proverbs 10:18; 20:19 (NASB)

He who conceals hatred has lying lips, and he who spreads slander is a fool.

He who goes about as a slanderer reveals secrets, therefore do not associate with a gossip.

1. What does a slanderer do?

2. Why is revealing secrets a wrong and hurtful thing to do?

3. This verse says not to even associate with a gossip. Is that a teaching you hear often from the pulpit or Christian books? Why do you think this isn't emphasized as much as other supposedly bigger sins?

4. Do you think God views some sins as bigger than others?

5. How should we feel about gossip and slander based on these verses?

6. How should this affect our own choice of words?

In an English country churchyard stands a drab, gray tombstone that bears an epitaph not easily seen unless you stoop over and look closely:

Beneath this stone, a lump of clay,
    lies Arabella Young,
who, on the twenty-fourth of May,
    began to hold her tongue.

Read Together Psalm 15:1-3 (NASB)

O LORD, who may abide in Your tent? Who may dwell on Your holy hill? He who walks with integrity, and works righteousness, and speaks truth in his heart. He does not slander with his tongue, nor does evil to his neighbor, nor takes up a reproach against his friend.

1. Who does this verse tell us can abide near to God?

2. What does "He...speaks truth in his heart" mean? Are these words spoken or unspoken?

3. Do the words in our hearts matter to God, or just the ones that escape our lips?

4. Why is it difficult for us to hold our tongue?

Read Together Job 32:21-22 (NASB)

Let me now be partial to no one, nor flatter any man. For I do not know how to flatter, else my Maker would soon take me away.

Flattery. This is also a subject we look at infrequently in discipleship and teaching. On the chart below, rate where you think our Christian culture is on viewing flattery as a sin—1 is a grievous sin, and 10 is no sin at all.

1-- 10

1. How is flattery used to manipulate?

2. Can you recall a time when someone was flattering to you until they got what they wanted—and their tone changed? How did you feel about this?

3. Why does flattery insult the character of God at such a deep level?

4. Read this excerpt from *Watch Your Mouth* and compare Judas's betrayal to flattery. Have you ever looked at Judas's kiss as a form of flattery? Does this affect the way you view this sin of flattery?

Flattery offers up sweet words, yet they come laced with the poison of manipulation. The purpose of flattery is always to gain favor. It is not a compliment given for the sake of expressing true appreciation. Rather, it is an intentional use of words to gain a position of advantage. Some people use flattery so often, they don't even notice they are doing it. They butter people up so they can use them for their own purposes. After all, most of us will respond to flattery. Who doesn't enjoy hearing compliments of how great we look, how well we do something, and the like?

Scripture has harsh words to say about the use of flattery. Jude writes about flattery in relation to false teachers when he says, "These are grumblers, finding fault, following after their own lusts; they speak arrogantly, flattering people for the sake of gaining an advantage" (Jude 16 NASB). Psalm 12 tells us that flatterers will be judged in the strictest of ways: "May the Lord cut off all flattering lips, the tongue that speaks great things" (Psalm 12:3 NASB). The Bible is letting us know that flattery is so damaging, manipulating, deceptive, and wrong that God would rather see the tongue removed altogether than allow it to continue.

Flattery is an insincere compliment designed to deceive the intended hearer or hearers in order to gain control over them. Flattery looks like a friend the same way a wolf looks like a dog. It may appear fluffy and cute, but it will rip you to shreds if you get close enough. It is Judas approaching Jesus with a kiss, a sign of affection, at the very moment of humanity's greatest betrayal.

Watch Your Mouth, pages 151–152

5. Are you aware of using flattery in your work, at home, or with friends? Will you ask God to make you aware if you are not? Take a moment to pray right now and ask for Him to make this clear to you.

Read Together 1 John 1:5-10 (NASB)

This is the message we have heard from Him and announce to you, that God is Light, and in Him there is no darkness at all. If we say that we have fellowship with Him and yet walk in the darkness, we lie and do not practice the truth; but if we walk in the Light as He Himself is in the Light, we have fellowship with one another, and the blood of

Jesus His Son cleanses us from all sin. If we say that we have no sin, we are deceiving ourselves and the truth is not in us. If we confess our sins, He is faithful and righteous to forgive us our sins and to cleanse us from all unrighteousness. If we say that we have not sinned, we make Him a liar and His word is not in us.

God is a God of truth and commands us to be people of truth.

Jesus was the only preacher who didn't seem to mind making His congregations smaller with His sermons. He would have big crowds following Him, and then He would come up with a line like "No one can come to Me unless it is granted to him by the Father" (John 6:65).

1. What happens in verse 66?

2. Why do you think that happened?

Jesus never let the crowd control the truth. He never flattered others, nor did He seek flattery. Likewise, out of His mouth came no manipulation, deception, or false witness. That's the same mouth that got a dead man up and out of a grave simply by saying his name. Do you want your lips to have the power to move mountains in your life and restore life to dead situations? Then let your lips be like Christ's in every way.

Read Together Ephesians 4:29 (NASB)

Let no unwholesome word proceed from your mouth, but only such a word as is good for edification according to the need of the moment, so that it will give grace to those who hear.

1. What does this verse say is not to proceed from our mouth?

2. List examples of everyday, common, unwholesome words.

3. What is to come out of our mouth instead?

4. List examples of words of edification.

5. How can our words give grace to those who hear them?

In Closing

So many of the people who feel free to praise God on Sunday feel just as free to laugh at filth the rest of the week. Free speech has become more important than clean speech.

Watch Your Mouth, page 156

As you end this session, consider how often you listen to gossip, slander, and filthy speech. Think about the news or television programs you watch and the video clips you see online. Would the things entering your ears honor God and please Him? Let this be a measurement for what you choose to watch and listen to.

As we conclude our study, complete the "On Your Own in the Coming Days" section below.

On Your Own in the Coming Days
Verses to Remember

As we saw with Travis in the video and the effect worship music had on the speech of one of the young men he mentored, countering negativity with positivity or lies with truth is a great approach. To counter any wrong in our mouths this week, commit to memory the following verses, all taken from the Psalms.

- "Lord, who can dwell in Your tent? Who can live on Your holy mountain? The one who lives honestly, practices righteousness, and acknowledges the truth in his heart—who does not slander with his tongue, who does not harm his friend or discredit his neighbor" (15:13).

- "You have tested my heart; You have examined me at night. You have tried me and found nothing evil; I have determined that my mouth will not sin" (17:3).

- "May the words of my mouth and the meditation of my heart be acceptable to You, Lord, my rock and my Redeemer" (19:14).

- "I said, 'I will guard my ways so that I may not sin with my tongue; I will guard my mouth with a muzzle as long as the wicked are in my presence'" (39:1).

- "Let the redeemed of the Lord proclaim that He has redeemed them from the hand of the foe" (107:2).

- "With my lips I proclaim all the judgments from Your mouth" (119:13).

- "Before a word is on my tongue, You know all about it, Lord" (139:4).

- "Lord, set up a guard for my mouth; keep watch at the door of my lips" (141:3).

Self-Analysis

Let's do a self-analysis on our speech. On the chart below, where 100 reflects complete self-control and holiness in speech and 0 reflects the other extreme, grade yourself with regard to the different areas we discussed in this lesson and in previous lessons. This will give you a visual on where you need to improve.

This may be even more helpful if you ask a close friend or relative to grade you as well. Then compare notes and set your mind on improving.

Encouraging and building up others

0------------------------------------- 50------------------------------------- 100

Speaking with wisdom

0------------------------------------- 50------------------------------------- 100

Praising God

0------------------------------------- 50------------------------------------- 100

Thanksgiving

0------------------------------------- 50------------------------------------- 100

Gossip

0------------------------------------- 50------------------------------------- 100

Putting others down or "cursing" others

0------------------------------------- 50------------------------------------- 100

Flattery

0------------------------------------- 50------------------------------------- 100

Filthy or rude speech

0------------------------------------- 50------------------------------------- 100

The Intentional Tongue

Pick a day this week to *notice* when you are saying or hearing anything negative. Choose to counter any negativity with five positive statements. This may feel awkward, but just try it for a day. It will heighten your awareness to negativity in you and around you. Be sure to include watching the news or listening to the radio.

Opening Your Mouth

What can you do to intentionally use your mouth to model to others what you have learned during the course of this study? Be careful not to beat anyone over the head, but follow the examples that Travis and Eloise's father provide—simply model a right heart that flows out of your mouth as a reflection of Christ in you.

Think about it, pray about it, and do it. Make it a lifestyle.

A Meditation

What have you been complaining about lately? What have you been using your mouth for that is contrary to the Lord's will for your life?

Take some serious time to mull this over, to pray, to feel, to confess, and to correct. Let the Holy Spirit speak to you and show you how Satan is using your own mouth against you. Then seek God and His strength to turn that around for good.

Appendix

Dr. Tony Evans
and The Urban Alternative

About Dr. Tony Evans

Dr. Tony Evans is founder and senior pastor of the 10,000-member Oak Cliff Bible Fellowship in Dallas, founder and president of The Urban Alternative, chaplain of the NBA's Dallas Mavericks, and author of many books, including *Destiny* and *Victory in Spiritual Warfare*. His radio broadcast, *The Alternative with Dr. Tony Evans*, can be heard on more than 1000 outlets and in more than 100 countries.

The Urban Alternative

The Urban Alternative (TUA) equips, empowers, and unites Christians to impact individuals, families, churches, and communities. TUA promotes a worldview that is thoroughly based on God's kingdom agenda. In teaching truth, we seek to transform lives.

The root of the problems we face in our personal lives, homes, churches, and societies is a spiritual one; therefore, the only way to address it is spiritually. We've tried political, social, economic, and religious agendas, but they have not brought lasting transformation.

> It's time for a kingdom agenda—the visible manifestation of the comprehensive rule of God over every area of life.

The unifying, central theme of the Bible is the glory of God through the advancement of His kingdom. This is the conjoining thread from Genesis to Revelation—from beginning to end. Without that theme, the Bible is a disconnected collection of stories that are inspiring but seem to be unrelated in purpose and direction. The Bible exists to share God's movement in history toward the establishment and expansion of His kingdom, highlighting the connectivity throughout which is the kingdom. This understanding increases the relevancy of these ancient writings to our day-to-day living because the kingdom is not only then; it is now.

The absence of the kingdom's influence in our own lives and in our families, churches, and communities has led to a catastrophic deterioration in our world.

- People live segmented, compartmentalized lives because they lack God's kingdom worldview.

- Families disintegrate because they exist for their own satisfaction rather than for the kingdom.

- Churches have limited impact because they fail to comprehend that the goal of the church is not the church itself, but the kingdom.

- Communities have nowhere to turn to find real solutions for real people who have real problems because the church has become divided, ingrown, and powerless to transform the cultural landscape in any relevant way.

The kingdom agenda offers us a way to live with a solid hope by optimizing the solutions of heaven. When God and His rule are not the final and authoritative standard over all, order and hope are lost. But the reverse is true as well—as long as we have God, we have hope. If God is still in the picture, and as long as His agenda is still on the table, it's not over.

Even if relationships collapse, God will sustain you. Even if finances dwindle, God will keep you. Even if dreams die, God will revive you. As long as God and His rule guide your life, family, church, and community, there is always hope.

Our world needs the King's agenda. Our churches need the King's agenda. Our families need the King's agenda.

In many major cities, drivers can take a loop to get to the other side of the city without driving straight through downtown. This loop takes them close enough to the city to see its towering buildings and skyline, but not close enough to actually experience it.

This is precisely what our culture has done with God. We have put Him on the "loop" of our personal, family, church, and community lives. He's close enough to be at hand should we need Him in an emergency, but too far away to be the center of who we are.

Sadly, we often want God on the "loop" of our lives, but we don't always want the King of the Bible to come downtown into the very heart of our ways. Leaving God on the "loop" brings about dire consequences, as we have seen in our own lives and with others. But when we make God and His rule the centerpiece of all we think, do, and say, we experience Him in the way He longs for us to.

He wants us to be kingdom people with kingdom minds set on fulfilling His kingdom purposes. He wants us to pray as Jesus did—"Not my will, but Thy will be done." Because His is the kingdom, the power, and the glory.

There is only one God, and we are not Him. As King and Creator, God calls the shots. Only when we align ourselves underneath His comprehensive hand will we access His full power and authority in our lives, families, churches, and communities.

As we learn how to govern ourselves under God, we will transform the institutions of family, church, and society according to a biblically based, kingdom worldview.

Under Him, we touch heaven and change earth.

To achieve our goal, we use a variety of strategies, approaches, and resources for reaching and equipping as many people as possible.

Broadcast Media

Millions of individuals experience *The Alternative with Dr. Tony Evans*, a daily broadcast playing on nearly 1000 radio outlets and in more than 100 countries. The broadcast can also be seen on several television networks, online at TonyEvans.org, and on the free Tony Evans app. More than four million message downloads occur each year.

Leadership Training

The *Tony Evans Training Center (TETC)* facilitates educational programming that embodies the ministry philosophy of Dr. Tony Evans as expressed through the kingdom agenda. The training courses focus on leadership development and discipleship in five tracks:

- Bible and theology
- personal growth
- family and relationships
- church health and leadership development
- society and community impact

The TETC program includes courses for both local and online students. Furthermore, TETC programming includes course work for nonstudent attendees. Pastors, Christian leaders, and Christian laity, both local and at a distance, can seek out the Kingdom Agenda Certificate for personal, spiritual, and professional development. Some courses qualify for continuing education credits and will transfer for college credit with our partner schools.

Kingdom Agenda Pastors (KAP) provides a viable network for like-minded pastors who embrace the kingdom agenda philosophy. Pastors have the opportunity to go deeper with Dr. Tony Evans as they are given greater biblical knowledge, practical applications, and resources to impact individuals, families, churches, and communities. KAP welcomes senior and associate pastors of all churches. KAP also offers an annual summit held each year in Dallas with intensive seminars, workshops, and resources.

Pastors' Wives Ministry, founded by Dr. Lois Evans, provides counsel, encouragement, and spiritual resources for pastors' wives as they serve with their husbands in the ministry. A primary focus of the ministry is the KAP Summit, which offers senior pastors' wives a safe place to reflect, renew, and relax along with training in personal development, spiritual growth, and care for their emotional and physical well-being.

Community Impact

National Church Adopt-A-School Initiative (NCAASI) empowers churches across the country to impact communities by using public schools as the primary vehicles for effecting positive social change in urban youth and families. Leaders of churches, school districts, faith-based organizations, and other nonprofit organizations are equipped with the knowledge and tools to forge partnerships and build strong social service delivery systems. This training is based on the comprehensive church-based community impact strategy conducted by Oak Cliff Bible Fellowship. It addresses such areas as economic development, education, housing, health revitalization, family renewal, and racial reconciliation. We assist churches in tailoring the model to meet specific needs of their communities while simultaneously addressing the spiritual and moral frame of reference. Training events are held annually in the Dallas area at Oak Cliff Bible Fellowship.

Athlete's Impact (AI) is an outreach into and through sports. Coaches are sometimes the most influential adults in young people's lives—even more so than parents. With the growing rise of fatherlessness in our culture, more young people are looking to their coaches for guidance, character development, practical needs, and hope. Athletes (professional or amateur) also influence younger athletes and kids. Knowing this, we aim to equip and train coaches and athletes to live out and utilize their God-given roles for the benefit of the kingdom. We aim to do this through our iCoach App, weCoach Football Conference, and other resources, such as *The Playbook: A Life Strategy Guide for Athletes*.

Resource Development

We are fostering lifelong learning partnerships with the people we serve by providing a variety of published materials. Dr. Evans has published more than 100 unique titles (booklets, books, and Bible studies) based on more than 40 years of preaching. The goal is to strengthen individuals in their walk with God and service to others.

For more information and a complimentary copy of Dr. Evans's devotional newsletter,

call
(800) 800-3222

or write
TUA
PO Box 4000
Dallas TX 75208

or visit our website
www.TonyEvans.org

More Great Harvest House Books
by Dr. Tony Evans

Watch Your Mouth

Your greatest enemy is actually in your mouth. Dr. Tony Evans reveals life-changing, biblical insights into the power of the tongue and how your words can be used to bless others or to usher in death. Be challenged to use your mouth to speak life into the world around you. (Also available—*Watch Your Mouth Growth and Study Guide.*)

A Moment for Your Soul

In this uplifting devotional, Dr. Evans offers a daily reading for Monday through Friday and one for the weekend—all compact, powerful, and designed to reach your deepest need. Each entry includes a relevant Scripture reading for the day. (eBook only)

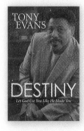

Destiny

Dr. Evans shows you the importance of finding your God-given purpose. He helps you discover and develop a custom-designed life that leads to the expansion of God's kingdom. Embracing your personal assignment from God will lead to your deepest satisfaction, God's greatest glory, and the greatest benefit to others.

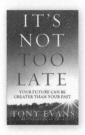

It's Not Too Late

Dr. Evans uses prominent Bible characters to show that God delights in using imperfect people who have failed, sinned, or just plain blown it. You'll be encouraged as you come to understand that God has you, too, on a path to success despite your imperfections and mistakes.

The Power of God's Names

Dr. Evans shows that it's through the names of God that the nature of God is revealed. By understanding the characteristics of God as revealed through His names, you will be better equipped to face the challenges life throws at you.

Praying Through the Names of God

Dr. Evans reveals insights into some of God's powerful names and provides prayers based on those names. Your prayer life will be revitalized as you connect your needs with the relevant characteristics of His names.

Victory in Spiritual Warfare

Dr. Evans demystifies spiritual warfare and empowers you with a life-changing truth: Every struggle faced in the physical realm has its root in the spiritual realm. With passion and practicality, Dr. Evans shows you how to live a transformed life in and through the power of Christ's victory.

Prayers for Victory in Spiritual Warfare

Feel defeated? God has given you powerful weapons to help you withstand the onslaught of Satan's lies. This book of prayers, based on Dr. Evans's life-changing book *Victory in Spiritual Warfare*, will help you stand against the enemy's attacks.

30 Days to Overcoming Emotional Strongholds

Dr. Evans identifies the most common and problematic emotional strongholds and demonstrates how you can break free from them—by aligning your thoughts with God's truth in the Bible.

30 Days to Victory Through Forgiveness

Has someone betrayed you? Are you suffering the consequences of your own poor choices? Or do you find yourself asking God, *Why did You let this happen?* Like a skilled physician, Dr. Tony Evans leads you through a step-by-step remedy that will bring healing to that festering wound and get you back on your journey to your personal destiny.

Horizontal Jesus

Do you want to sense God's encouragement, comfort, and love for you every day? Dr. Tony Evans reveals that as you live like a horizontal Jesus—giving these things away to others—you will personally experience them with God like never before. (Also available—*Horizontal Jesus Study Guide.*)

To learn more about Harvest House books and
to read sample chapters, visit our website:

www.harvesthousepublishers.com

HARVEST HOUSE PUBLISHERS
EUGENE, OREGON